MW00983288

The First Dish

Authentic Peasant Recipes From Little Italy

Angel Marinaccio

Silver Spring

Published in the United States by
Beckham Publications Group, Inc.
P.O. Box 4066, Silver Spring, MD 20914

ISBN: 978-0-9848243-9-7

Library of Congress Control Number: 2012943196

DEDICATION

When I decided to write this cookbook, I reached out to all my family and friends and asked them for their favorite First Dish Recipes. It got us talking and reminiscing on how their mom, dad, or grandma made that certain dish and how it is still made today in their homes.

I dedicate this book to them, and honor the generations before them that passed down these wonderful, authentic Italian recipes.

In the movie *It's a Wonderful Life,* Clarence the angel left a book for George to remember him by. He wrote this message inside:

"No Man Is a Failure Who Has Friends."

I believe those words are true. My family and friends are always there for me. I wouldn't have been able to write this cookbook without them.

I hope you enjoyed all these great recipes. Now . . . start cooking!

I'll see you soon at my table.

–Angel

TO MY HUSBAND LOUIS

My Soul Mate:

Sometimes I think back on the years when we were beginning our lives together. We were just teenagers when we got married, raising two children. It was hard for both of us. But we made it through those times, with the strength we gave each other.

You are my friend, my love, my everything. I can't imagine sharing my life with anyone but you. Forever and always my heart belongs to you. I love you.

These Two Little Words—Thank You—mean more than you'll ever know! I feel very privileged to have such good people around me, to help me along the way. So, with gratitude, I say, Thank You!

To my son Gerard and his wife Lola, thank you for helping me with the cover and designing the chapters in the book.

To Reece, thank you for all your help and patience with your computer skills. As always, you're there for me.

To my family and friends, thank you for all the great recipes.

Keep on cooking!

To Emilio from Ballato Ristorante Italiano, thank you so much for letting me take pictures of the stove that's in the window of Ballato's Restaurant for the cover of the book and for a wonderful tasting party.

Thank you, Daniel Akselrad, a student at NYU. He did a great job taking the pictures at the tasting party. What a gentleman!

Last, but not least, to Charles Messina, thank you always.

Menu

The First Dish

These recipes are old-world dishes that were handed down from one generation to another, keeping with the traditions of our homeland.

From Italy to Little Italy, enjoy the taste of my authentic peasant dishes.

Growing up in Little Italy with all its wonderful stores to shop in was a plus. It was and still is a great place to live. Mott Street back then is today's Union Square market with all the fresh fruit and vegetables. We had butcher shops, pork stores, and fish stores. Bakeries like Parisi's and, of course, our famous Di Palo's Cheese Store, are still there and going strong to this day. What more did we need? They were all at our doorstep.

The smells when you walked down the street were amazing. In the summertime, the Greek on the corner of Mott and Grand Street would have olives in baskets outside his store, along with babaluge (snails) that were crawling out of the baskets. He also sold spices, dried beans, chestnuts, and olive oil. The watermelon truck would come by, and the man would yell out, "watermelon." You could buy half a melon for 50 cents. The Sicilian pizza was in a glass case outside Dino Maggiore's bread store. Oh boy! I loved to shop for my mom, grandma, or any family member. I ate my way down the street.

In the winter, an old man with his chestnut cart passed by. Every time I smell chestnuts roasting it brings me back to those days and reminds me of that old man. I love that smell to this day. There was even a knish man who also sold out of a cart. He was dressed with a long coat, scarf, hat, and gloves that were cut so his fingers could be out to count the money you handed him. I guess he was the first to start that trend. He handed you the knish in a brown bag after he salted and shook the bag.

It was great.

Thinking back when I was a kid, at dinnertime, whatever our parents or grandma put on the table for dinner we ate with no question. We didn't have a choice in the matter back then. I must say we all survived. In the morning when I woke up for breakfast, the ladies in my building would be talking to each other in the hallways or through their windows in the courtyard of my building. I would hear them say, "What are you cooking tonight?" and they would ask each other, "When I go shopping, do you need anything?" That's how it was back then. They didn't even finish their coffee or swallow their breakfast before they got started. The menu was done for the day and these dishes were prepared in every household. The family would fill up on the first dish (primo piatto) because it was an inexpensive meal to make.

The first dish consisted of an antipasta (hot or cold appetizer), a vegetable, brodo (soup), pasta dishes, omelet (frittata), meat, or fish. Oh, how I love them all! There were times in my house we would only eat the first dish, but what great meals they were. I love all those old-world recipes, and I still make them today.

In my neighborhood, people enjoy dishes from all over Italy. We are Sicilian, Neapolitan, Calabrese, and Barese. We live in Little Italy and cook our traditional regional dishes. We are one, but we are different in our cooking.

My family and friends are great cooks. They can whip up a first dish in no time. These are their recipes. Enjoy them.

After reading and making all these fabulous recipes, the only thing you will need is a great piece of Italian bread. *Mangia!*

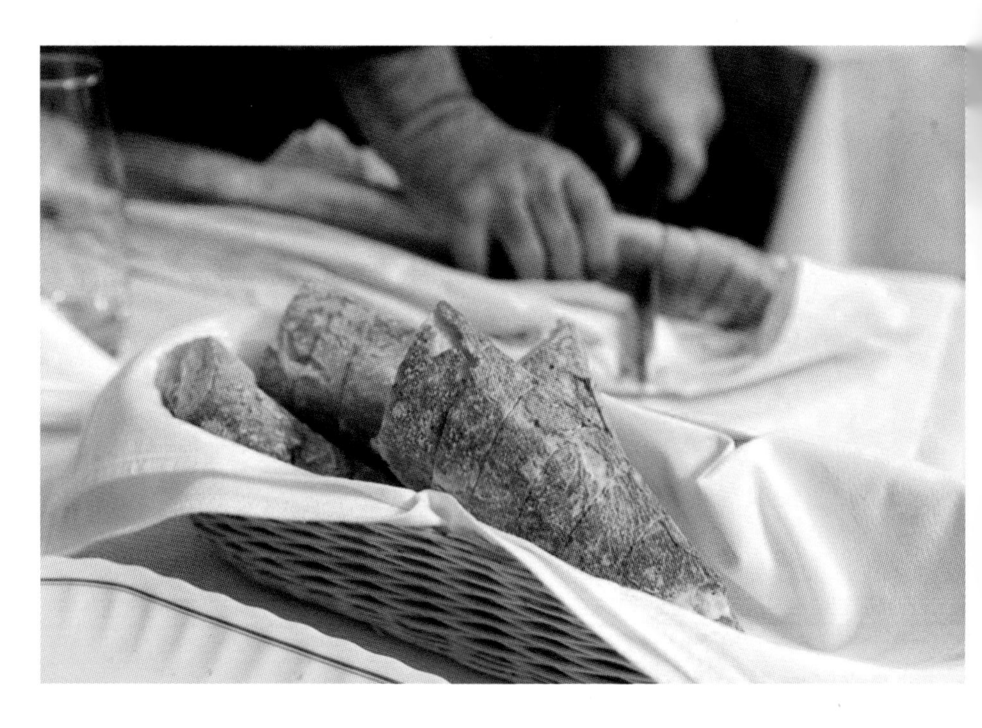

MY grandma always said:

"If you have garlic and oil, you can make anything," and with my recipes you can.

Antipasti

MASI
ANTIPASTI

COLD ANTIPASTA

This dish is so simple to make, I love it.

I shop at Di Palo's in NYC's Little Italy, my favorite store. Many of these same ingredients can also be found in your local market in the Italian section of the store.

- 1 large mozzarella, thinly sliced
- 2 large tomatoes, thinly sliced
- 1 large jar roasted peppers, sliced, or fresh roasted peppers, sliced
- 1 jar marinated artichoke hearts, drained
- black olives, pitted
- olive oil
- salt
- pepper
- basil

On a platter, place a slice of tomato, top with a slice of mozzarella, a slice of roasted pepper, and then the artichoke hearts. Continue this pattern, fill the dish with all the ingredients, then add some black olives. Sprinkle some olive oil over the top. Add salt, pepper, and basil to taste. If you like anchovies, place them on the side.

This dish is made all the time in my house, for any occasion. Serve with Italian bread.

For an extra surprise that will delight your palate, have a bowl of ricotta on the table. Place a spoon of ricotta on a piece of Italian bread and drizzle a little honey on top. Wow!

STUFFED ARTICHOKES

During the holidays or for a special dinner, you would find stuffed artichokes on my dinner table. It shows your guests that you took time to make them something special.

- 8 medium or large artichokes
- 3 cups Italian-style bread crumbs
- 4 pieces garlic, chopped
- ½ cup cheese
- salt
- pepper
- parsley
- olive oil

When buying an artichoke, it should not look dry, or if a leaf comes off when pulled, don't buy it. Cut off the bottom so it can stand, then cut off the tip of each leaf with kitchen scissors so there are no points. At the top, make an even cut with a knife. Then, open up the artichoke real wide with your hand so there will be room to stuff it. Wash them good and place them in a colander to drain.

Combine all the ingredients in a bowl, and then slowly add olive oil so it becomes a paste. Add more bread crumbs or cheese, if needed. This mixture is called oreganatta. Stuff the center and between the leaves with the mixture.

For eight artichokes, use two large pots, four in each. Add water slowly with a cup, halfway up the side so the water won't touch the top of the artichoke. Add olive oil and garlic to the water. Cover the pots and cook them on a low to medium flame. The artichokes are cooked if you can pull a leaf off it very easily. Place the artichokes on a platter and eat at room temperature.

Eat slowly so you can enjoy every sumptuous leaf.

STUFFED MUSHROOMS

When making hot antipasta, I always add stuffed mushrooms to the dish and during the holidays, you'll find them on my table as a great side dish for turkey on Thanksgiving or ham on Christmas Day.

- 1 large box mushrooms, or 2 small boxes, washed and stems cut off
- 1½ cups bread crumbs (Italian style or plain)
- 4 tablespoons Parmesan cheese
- 2 cloves chopped garlic
- Italian parsley chopped fine or dried parsley
- salt
- pepper
- olive oil

Preheat the oven to 350 degrees.

Combine all dried ingredients in a bowl, and add the olive oil slowly. It will become a paste. This is called oreganata.

In a greased pan, place the mushrooms faceup. Stuff the mushrooms with a spoonful of the mixture.

Bake until golden brown. Place on a platter and eat at room temperature.

You'll taste all the delicious ingredients with each bite you take of the stuffed mushrooms. It is like eating potato chips; you can't stop with one. Enjoy these delicious little bundles.

MY DAUGHTER ANN MARIE'S FAVORITE—MOZZARELLA CARROZZA

The name means "mozzarella in a carriage." The carriage is the bread. This dish is easy to make.

- Italian bread sliced or whatever bread you prefer
- mozzarella cheese, sliced
- 1½ cups Italian-style bread crumbs
- 1 egg beaten with a drop of milk
- less than ½ cup olive oil

When the bread and the mozzarella are sliced make it into a sandwich.

In a bowl, beat the egg, then place the bread crumbs in a dish. Now you ready to start.

In a medium-size pan, heat the oil on a low to medium flame.

Dip the sandwich into the egg, then the bread crumbs. Then fry them. When golden brown, turn and fry on the other side. Place on a platter.

Some serve this dish with a side of tomato sauce to dip the mozzarella carrozza. I love it just like that with all the mozzarella melted.

My daughter has loved this dish since she was a little girl.

SIS URSULA STUFFED BELL PEPPERS

Ursula is quite a cook. She takes after my mother-in-law Gracie.

- 6 large red bell peppers
- 1½ cups plain bread crumbs
- 6 cloves garlic, finely chopped
- 1 small jar capers in vinegar
- Salt
- pepper
- olive oil to moisten the bread crumbs

Preheat the oven to 350 degrees.

Cut the peppers in half, remove all the seeds and veins, and rinse with cold water. Drain the vinegar from the capers and rinse well with water.

Combine bread crumbs, garlic, capers, salt, and pepper to taste in a large bowl, then drizzle with olive oil until moist.

Stuff the mixture into the peppers and place them on a greased pan and bake until the peppers are soft and the bread crumbs are slightly brown, for 25 to 30 minutes.

Serve as a side dish or as a hot antipasto.

Ursula is not only a great cook, she's also a great baker. During the holidays, we can't wait for her to make struffoli and her Christmas Eve fish dinner rocks.

AUNT MINNIE'S PEPPER MEDLEY

This is a great first dish. It's easy and fast to make.

- 4 red bell peppers, cleaned and cut into quarters
- 2 cans black pitted olive, drained
- 1 small jar capers, drained
- 2 cups bread crumbs, seasoned or plain
- ½ cup olive oil

After cutting the peppers, place the olive oil in a pan and start frying the peppers. Add the olives and capers when they start to become soft. Mix together. Cook for 10 minutes more.

In another frying pan, toast the bread crumbs. Place the pepper mixture on a platter and top it with toasted bread crumbs.

Sometimes all you need is a simple little recipe like Aunt Minnie's Pepper Medley for a first dish or as a side with any meal you make. It's delicious!

COUSIN PHYLLIS'S EGGPLANT ROLLATINI

- 1 large eggplant
- 1 pound ricotta
- ½ pound mozzarella
- salt
- pepper
- olive oil
- 1 28-ounce can crushed tomatoes
- 1 medium onion
- 2 cloves garlic, chopped
- parsley

Preheat the oven to 350 degrees.

Cut off the ends of the eggplant, then peel the skin. Thinly slice the eggplant lengthwise. Rinse with salt water to remove the bitterness, then pat dry with paper towels. Place in a large saucepan and add the olive oil. Cook on medium heat. When hot, add the eggplant and fry until golden brown. Remove from the pan and place on a dish with paper towels to drain some of the oil.

Cut the mozzarella into small thin slices, place in a bowl, add ricotta, salt, and pepper to taste, and mix it all together. When the eggplant is cool, spoon the mixture in the center of the eggplant and spread it, then roll it. When you finish rolling, set the eggplant aside.

To make marinara sauce, add the oil, onions, and garlic in a pan and cook to golden, then add the tomatoes. Cook on a low to medium heat for half an hour; stir occasionally. You can use marinara sauce or meat sauce with this dish.

In a baking pan, add some sauce, place the eggplant rollatini on it, add more sauce on top, then some grated cheese and parsley. Bake for half an hour. Remove from the oven when the mozzarella is melted.

This dish is delicious as a main course or a side dish with pasta.

This is great, just like my cousin Phyllis.

CAPONATA

This is our family favorite! My cousins Ernie and Betty make it great.

- 3 medium or large eggplants cut into ½ inch pieces (leave skin on)
- 2 7-ounce jars stuffed green olives
- 2 15-ounce cans black olives
- 1 2½ ounce jar capers (optional)
- 4 28-ounce cans Tuttorosso crushed tomatoes
- 5 to 6 pieces chopped garlic
- 3 onions, sliced and then cut in quarters
- ½ cup onion, finely chopped
- Stalk of celery cut up in 1-inch pieces
- ½ cup olive oil
- 3 packets Sweet'N Low sugar

Prepare the sauce:

Heat the olive oil in a large saucepot. Add onions and the chopped garlic and brown. Then add four cans of crushed tomatoes. Simmer for 45 minutes.

Add eggplant, celery, onions, black olives, green olives, and capers. This MUST cook for about 4 hours on a low flame. The longer it cooks, the better it is so the eggplant and celery become soft. After about 3 hours, add this very special ingredient, three packets of Sweet'N Low sugar. Stir well. It removes the bitterness and adds some sweetness to it. Simmer 1 more hour, stirring constantly. Do not let it burn or stick to the bottom of the pot.

This can be served as an appetizer or over a bowl of rigatoni. Mmmm good!

This dish takes time. The most important ingredient is love. When my cousins make Caponata, we all bring our bowls with us so we can take some home.

MY COUSIN BABY PHYLLIS'S FAMOUS RICE BALLS

- 1 pound Carolina rice or any other rice
- 4 eggs
- ¾ cup grated cheese
- salt
- 1 15-ounce can tomato sauce and add 1 can water
- ½ pound chopped meat
- 1 small can peas
- 2 cups bread crumbs

Separate the eggs and set the yoke aside. You can use this to dip the rice balls in when you are preparing to fry them.

In a small frying pan, add some olive oil and brown the chopped meat, then drain and put to the side.

Add tomato sauce, water, chopped meat, and peas in a saucepan and cook for 15 minutes.

Boil rice in a large pot. The rice should absorb all the water. Once it thickens, add the four egg whites and keep stirring. Add the grated cheese slowly while continuing to stir. Add a little of the tomato sauce without any meat or peas in it for color. It is now ready to be placed in a pan to cool. Once it is fully cooled, take a handful of rice and separate it. Place a little sauce, meat, and peas in the middle and layer more rice on top, making it into a ball. Dip it into the egg yoke and roll in bread crumbs. Fry. You can make 12 to 18 rice balls depending on the size. Once you start eating them you can't stop.

Baby Phil will always have a special place in my heart. We love her.

CAROL'S STUFFED PEPPERS

To make these fabulous stuffed peppers, you'll need a total of two pounds of chopped beef, pork, and veal. These meats are in your local market or butcher shop.

- 4 extra large red peppers, washed, remove the seeds, and cut in half
- 2 pounds total chopped beef, pork, and veal
- 1 cup uncooked Minute Rice
- 4 tablespoons Italian grated cheese
- 1 teaspoon garlic powder
- salt
- pepper
- 1 bottle Kraft's Catalina salad dressing
- 1 small can Del Monte tomato sauce
- olive oil

Preheat oven at 400 degrees.

Combine the meat, the uncooked Minute Rice, grated cheese, salt and pepper to taste, garlic powder, and salad dressing in a bowl. Mix well, then place to the side till needed.

Wash the peppers and cut in half, then stuff with the mixture. Place in a roasting pan that is coated on the bottom with olive oil. Pour the tomato sauce over the peppers. Bake in the oven for 1 hour. Stuffed peppers are great as a side dish or as hot antipasti.

Carol has a very busy life, but she always finds time to make her fabulous stuffed peppers.

ZUCCHINI ESCARPESCE (FRIED ZUCCHINI WITH OLIVE OIL AND BALSAMIC VINEGAR)

- 4 small or medium zucchini
- ½ cup olive oil
- 3 cloves garlic, chopped
- 5 tablespoons balsamic vinegar
- salt
- pepper
- fresh or dried parsley flakes

Wash the zucchini well. Cut the ends off and discard, but keep the skin on. Slice the zucchini thin into round circles. In a pan, heat the olive oil on a low to medium flame. When hot, add the zucchini and fry on both sides until golden brown.

After frying, place in a large bowl and add a little more olive oil, balsamic vinegar, and season with salt and pepper to taste. Slice the garlic and add to the zucchini with some parsley.

You can serve zucchini escarpesce warm or cold. This dish is great as a appetizer or a side dish

POTATO PANCAKES

This is my cousin Jill's favorite dish to make. Potato pancakes are great to serve as an appetizer with a little caviar and crème fraise or as a side dish with applesauce. This is a family recipe passed down by my grandmother Florence. It is fairly simple because we've modernized it.

The key to this recipe is preparing your potato mixture in batches, which allows for the right ratio of seasonings and keeps the potatoes from discoloring before you fry them. This combo makes one batch, which will make about a dozen small pancakes. I can easily make several batches in one night because my family eats them as they come out of the pan.

- 3 medium Idaho potatoes
- 1 medium to large onion
- 1 egg
- Matzo Meal (you can substitute with bread crumbs, but I like to stick with tradition)
- salt
- pepper

Grate the potatoes and the onion in a food processor using a grater attachment that will give you long shreds as if you used an old-fashioned handheld grater. Spoon the grated mixture into a bowl and run your fingers through it, removing any pieces that feel too big. Put them through the processer again or discard.

Now that your potato/onion mixture is grated roughly the same size, stir in the egg and a liberal sprinkling of Matzo Meal to absorb any excess liquid and bind the mixture. Add salt and pepper to taste. My grandmother would call it "a pinch" of each, but it's probably about ¼ teaspoon of salt and ⅛ teaspoon of pepper. Add more or less as needed. The consistency should be wet and thick, but because the potatoes will expel water, feel free to add a little more Matzo Meal to the mixture at any time.

Heat Canola oil in a frying pan or cast-iron skillet. The oil must be very hot. Test it with a little piece of potato mixture. Use a soup spoon to measure medium-size (2-3 inch) pancakes. Add a scoop of the mixture to the hot oil and gently press the center mound down to flatten the pancake. Cook a few minutes on each side so that they're crispy brown on the outside, but soft and cooked on the inside. When you are finished frying the potato pancakes, place on a platter and serve.

This is a great first dish to serve for any holiday. I think it's wonderful that Jill is keeping the tradition alive with her grandma Florence's recipe. That's what it's all about.

LINDA'S INCREDIBLE FIORI DI ZUCCHINI (ZUCCHINI BLOSSOMS)

- 12 zucchini blossoms, stems and pistils removed
- 1 cup self-rising flour
- 5 eggs
- 1¼ tablespoons Locatelli Romano cheese
- salt
- pepper
- olive oil or vegetable oil

If you want, try stuffing them with goat cheese or mozzarella, and then follow the instructions for the recipe.

In a bowl, add beaten eggs, Locatelli Romano cheese, and flour. Season with salt and pepper to taste. Wash and pat dry the zucchini blossoms. Heat the oil for frying. Dredge the blossoms in the flour mixture and place them individually in the frying pan. Fry until golden brown. Serve on a platter.

Linda's grandma had a vegetable garden, and in the summer she grew zucchini with its blossoms. Linda remembers her grandmother gathering all the grandchildren to pick the blossoms from the zucchini, then she would prepare this delicious delicacy.

POTATO CROQUETTES

Joe and Cathy's Specialty!

- 3 pounds potatoes
- 2 egg yolks (reserve whites in a bowl)
- ½ pound Locatelli grated cheese
- 1 pound Polly-O mozzarella, shredded
- 1 cup chopped parsley
- 1 cup bread crumbs
- 1 cup vegetable oil
- salt
- pepper

Boil the potatoes until tender. Strain water and peel skins when the potatoes are cool. Mash potatoes, then add egg yolk, cheese, mozzarella, parsley, salt and pepper to taste. Mix everything with your hands. Spoon the mixture into your hands and roll to make a croquette form. Dip in egg whites and cover with bread crumbs. Fry croquettes until golden brown on all sides.

Place on a dish and serve.

Joe and Cathy are a sweet and wonderful couple, and I am very happy to have them in my life.

Brodo

SOUP

SOUP

PASTA FAGIOLI (WHITE BEAN SOUP)

When my cousin Marylou makes this dish, it draws a crowd.

- 3 cans cannellini beans (white kidney beans) or dried beans (cook first, and then add all the ingredients)
- 3 pieces garlic, cut up
- 2 celery stalks, cut up into small pieces
- 1 small can Del Monte tomato sauce, plain
- 8 tablespoons olive oil
- salt
- pepper
- crushed red pepper (optional)
- pasta

In a medium to large pot, cook the garlic, and celery in olive oil over a medium flame until it is a golden color, then add the tomato sauce and simmer until it starts to bubble. Add the beans (my cousin prefers canned beans with ½ can of water for each can of beans). Mix together, then season with salt and pepper to taste, and crushed red pepper (if desired). Cook for 30 to 45 minutes. You know it's done when the smell is great!

Boil your pasta and add salt to the water. When it is cooked, place a small pot under the strainer when you drain the pasta, so you can reserve some of the pasta water, which you might need later. Place the pasta in a bowl, add the cannellini bean mixture, then mix all together. If it becomes too dried, add some pasta water.

I love pasta Fagioli with a bag or box of small mix macaroni or broken spaghette. This dish is made all yearlong in Marylou's house. We love it.

THE WEDDING SOUP

This soup was a tradition long ago at Italian weddings. That's how it got its name. The soup is made all the time now. Nashie makes it the best, but now the celebration is the soup.

- 2 heads escarole or fresh spinach or 2 boxes frozen chopped spinach (whichever you prefer)
- 2 cloves garlic
- 2 tablespoons olive oil
- 96 fluid ounces of chicken stock (clear, fresh, boxed, or canned)
- ½ pound beef, chopped
- ½ box Orzo pasta
- salt
- pepper
- dried parsley
- grated cheese
- garlic powder

Wash the spinach or escarole. Boil the vegetable of your choice with the 2 cloves of garlic till tender in a pot of water that just covers the greens. When done, remove the greens from the water and put aside. Add the olive oil, salt, and pepper to taste. If you are using frozen spinach, cook till tender, then add the garlic, salt, pepper, and olive oil. In a medium to large pot, add the chicken stock and greens. Do not put the garlic in the soup. Simmer on a low to medium flame.

In a bowl, mix the chopped meat with three tablespoons of cheese, one teaspoon of parsley, salt and pepper to taste, and two shakes of garlic powder. Mix. With a tablespoon, scoop out some of the mixture and roll into small meatballs. Continue till all is done. When the soup is almost to a boil, add the meatballs. Cook for 35 minutes.

Boil the Orzo pasta in salted water, and then add to the soup. Cook for 5 more minutes. Place in a bowl. Sprinkle grated cheese on top.

Oh boy! You'll be dancing the tarantella as if you were at an Italian wedding after you eat this delicious soup.

JOJO'S MINESTRONE SOUP (VEGETABLE SOUP)

This soup is an Italian specialty, and Jojo make this minestrone soup all the time, just like her grandma.

- ¼ cup olive oil
- 1 large onion, chopped
- 1 garlic clove, chopped
- 1 carrot, peeled and sliced
- 2 celery stalks, sliced
- 1 box frozen broccoli or 1 head fresh broccoli
- 1 box frozen cauliflower or 1 head fresh cauliflower
- 1 box frozen or fresh spinach or 1 head of escarole
- 1 can each corn, peas, and white beans
- 2 large cans or 2 boxes beef stock
- 2 zucchini, washed and sliced
- salt
- pepper
- 1 tablespoon Italian seasoning
- 2 tablespoons parmigiano cheese

Place the oil in a large pot. Sauté the onions, carrots, celery, and garlic over a medium flame until tender. If using frozen vegetables, defrost first; if using fresh vegetables, wash and add to the pot. Sauté the broccoli, cauliflower, and zucchini until tender. Add the beef stock; fill the pot three-fourths full. Boil, then add the spinach or escarole. Cover the pot and simmer for 1 hour.

Drain the canned vegetables and add them to the pot as well as all the seasonings. Cook for 20 minutes longer. Serve in a large bowl and sprinkle the parmigiano cheese on top. One bowl contains a week's worth of vegetables. Wow!

Jojo, she's special in our life. We love her.

COUSIN DONNA'S BEEF SOUP

- carrots
- celery
- onion
- parsley
- beef of your choice (I use bottom round)
- 2 or 3 beef bones
- 1 small can tomato sauce
- salt
- pepper
- pasta

In a large pot cover the beef and bones with water. Boil for approximately 5 minutes. Discard the water and fill the pot with fresh water almost to the top. Add all the vegetables (whole) and the tomato sauce. Bring to a boil, then simmer for 2 to 2½ hours.

When the soup is ready, transfer the broth to another pot and cook the pasta in the broth. When done, place the soup in large bowl on the table, shred the beef, and place on a platter along with the vegetables for all to take.

I love acini di pepe pasta with this beef soup. I'm a chicken soup lover. I never made beef soup until Cousin Donna shared her recipe with me.

Donna's beef soup is great. Try this recipe. I think you'll agree.

MARIE GUGS'S (MINESTRA) SOUP

Marie Gugs is the mother of my friends Augusta, Lucille, Anthony & Maria. She had a heart of gold.

- 1 pound chopped beef
- 1 medium onion, chopped
- ¼ cup olive oil
- 2 potatoes, peeled and diced
- 2 medium carrots, peeled and diced
- 1 bag frozen peas
- 4 hard-boiled eggs (peel and set aside)
- 1½ cups white rice (or 2 bags instant rice)
- 1 small can Del Monte tomato sauce
- salt
- pepper
- 2 cans water

Heat the olive oil in a large pot on a medium to low flame. Sauté the onions until golden brown. Add the chopped meat. Break the meat apart with a spoon so that it is even on the bottom of the pot. When the meat is brown, add the tomato sauce, 2 cans of water, salt and pepper to taste, and stir. Cook until it starts bubbling, then add the potatoes and carrots and mix together. When the potatoes are tender, add the frozen peas and the hard-boiled eggs. Cook for another 15 minutes. Spoon the minestra over a bed of white rice in a large bowl.

This dish was made back in the day when the moms knew how to stretch a meal. Marie Gugs, I'll never forget your kindness.

COUSIN DAWN'S SPLIT PEA (MINESTRA) SOUP

Dawn is my cousin Nancy Ann's daughter. She is the fourth generation still cooking old-world recipes in my family.

- 1 bag dried peas
- 1 medium onion, sliced thin
- 2 tablespoons butter
- 2 carrots, sliced thin
- 3 celery stalks, diced
- 2 medium potatoes, diced
- salt
- pepper
- 1 ham bone or shank
- 1 box chicken broth or 8 cups chicken broth

When opening the bag of dried peas you should always rinse them in a dish twice to make sure they are clean. Place the butter, onion, carrots, celery, salt and pepper to taste in a large pot and cook for 7 to 10 minutes. Then add all the rest of the ingredients. Add water to almost reach the top of the pot. Cover and cook for 1½ hours on a low to medium fame.

Remove the ham bone from the soup. You can puree the soup in a blender if you like or just serve as is. Toss some croutons into your bowl of soup. Delicious.

You'll love this split pea soup just like I do.

PASTA E LENTICCHIE (MACARONI WITH LENTILS)

- 1 bag dried lentils
- 4 carrots
- 2 celery stalks
- 1 medium onion
- 1 garlic clove
- slightly less than ¼ cup olive oil
- pasta

Examine the lentils on a dish for stones, then rinse the lentils in cold water.

Chop 2 carrots, 2 celery sticks, 1 onion, and 1 garlic clove. In a large pot, heat the oil. Add the chopped vegetables to the pan and stir. Simmer for 5 minutes. Add the lentils and fill the pot with water almost to the top.

Cut the 2 remaining carrots into small pieces and add them to the lentils and cook for 1½ hours on a low to medium flame. Stir occasionally. The soup will become thick. Season with salt and pepper to taste. I love cut spaghetti with this dish. You can cook it in the lentils soup or cook it separately. You can also add rice instead of pasta. It's great with this dish.

I've eaten pasta lenticchie all my life, but I must say, my friend Nancy is up there along with my grandma as cooking some of the best I ever tasted.

ESSCOLI & BEANS

- 2 large heads esscoli
- 3 garlic cloves, chopped
- ¼ cup olive oil
- 2 large cans cannellini beans, red or white
- salt
- pepper
- rice

Cut the end off the esscoli and discard. Wash the esscoli well. It may have some sand so rinse all the leaves, then cut in half and place in a pot. Cover the esscoli with salted water. Cook on medium flame until tender. When done, remove the esscoli from the pot with half of the water and place in a bowl until needed. Discard the rest of water from the pot.

Heat the olive oil in the pot, then add garlic and cook until golden brown. Add the beans, esscoli, salt and pepper to taste. Stir. Cook for 20 minutes on a low flame.

You can cook rice and place some on the bottom of your dish, then cover with esscoli and beans. Season with dried crushed red pepper on top for some extra "heat."

This dish is made all the time in my house. We love it!

MY CHICKEN SOUP

Grandma Fanny taught me how to make this great soup.

- 2 skinless chicken legs
- 2 skinless chicken breasts
- 2 bags carrots, peeled
- 1 large onion, peeled
- 5 celery stalks, washed and peeled
- 1 large potato
- a handful fresh parsley
- 1 small can Del Monte tomato sauce (use only 2 tablespoons)
- salt
- pepper
- Orzo pasta or rice

Wash all the ingredients, then place them in a large pot. Fill the pot with water, and add salt and pepper to taste. Cover the pot and cook on medium heat until it starts to boil, then lower the flame and cook for 2 hours. Remove all the ingredients and place in a dish.

In a blender, add at least 4 carrots, all the celery, half of the onion, parsley, and some of the broth. Puree, then add the puree mixture to the soup and stir.

Shred the chicken, slice the carrots and the rest of the onion, and add to the soup. Season with salt and pepper to taste. Ladle the soup into bowls.

You can cook Orzo pasta or rice on the side, and add it to the soup when cooked.

I love making this soup on a cold winter's day.

PASTA

PASTA

PASTA

PASTA AGLIO E OLIO (PASTA WITH GARLIC & OIL)

This simple dish is made all the time in our house. It is my favorite.

Start with thin spaghetti boiling in a pot. When it's almost done, prepare your mixture.

- 4 large cloves garlic, chopped into small pieces
- a handful fresh parsley, finely chopped
- 1 cup olive oil
- crushed red pepper (optional)
- grated cheese
- thin spaghetti

In a medium pot, place all the ingredients except the spaghetti and cheese. Add salt, pepper, and crushed red pepper to taste. Cook on a low flame. When the garlic becomes translucent, it's done. Move the pot to the side.

Boil the pasta, then strain it in a colander. Place a small pot underneath it to hold some of the pasta water. Place the pasta in a bowl, then mix all the ingredients together. Add some pasta water if it becomes dry. Top it off with cheese.

This recipe is so easy. It has many spin-offs just by adding different ingredients to the dish. Be creative!

(AGLIO E OLIO) PASTA WITH GARLIC AND OIL

From this simple recipe you can make great dishes by adding these extra ingredients Broccoli and Cavatelli.

- 1 bunch broccoli or 1 bag or box frozen broccoli
- 4 cloves garlic, chopped
- ½ cup olive oil
- 1 pound cavatelli pasta
- salt
- pepper
- grated cheese

If using fresh broccoli, wash and cut it. If using frozen broccoli, defrost slightly before adding it to the warm garlic and oil.

Place the broccoli in a pan with garlic and oil. Season with salt and pepper to taste. Cook on a medium flame.

Boil salted water, then add the cavatelli pasta. Cook until al dente. Strain the pasta over a small pot, reserving some pasta water in case you need it later if the mixture is too dry.

Mix all the ingredients together in a bowl, then sprinkle some grated cheese on top.

Now that's a great dish. If you can't find cavatelli pasta, rigatoni will do.

PASTA PRIMAVERA WITH CAPELLINI (THE FIRST VEGETABLES OF SPRING)

- 1 bag frozen mixed vegetable or fresh vegetables
- garlic
- oil
- capellini pasta
- salt
- pepper
- grated cheese

You can use fresh seasonal vegetables or a simple bag of frozen mix. When using fresh vegetables, wash them thoroughly, then cut them to the size you desire. When using frozen vegetables, slightly thaw first before adding the vegetables to warm oil.

Sauté all the vegetables in a pan with garlic and oil. Season with salt and pepper to taste.

Boil salted water, then add the capellini pasta. When done, strain the pasta over a small pot, reserving some pasta water in case you need it later if the mixture becomes too dry.

Mix all ingredients together in a bowl and sprinkle some grated cheese on top. A great summer dish.

BROCCOLI RABE WITH SAUSAGE OVER ORECCHIETTE PASTA

Either pork or chicken sausage works best with this recipe.

- 6 pieces sausage
- 1 large head broccoli rabe or 2 small heads broccoli
- 1 cup olive oil
- 4 cloves garlic
- 1 box Orecchiette pasta
- salt
- pepper
- grated cheese

Bake the sausage until well done or fry the sausage in some olive oil. Slice it into round pieces and set aside. Wash the broccoli rabe to remove any sand. Cut the ends off and discard, but keep the flowers and the stems. Cook in a pan with garlic and oil and cover until it's tender. Add the cooked sausage. Season with salt and pepper to taste.

Boil Orecchiette in salted water. Strain the pasta over a small pot, reserving some pasta water to use to moisten the mixture if it becomes too dry.

Mix all ingredients together, place on a serving platter, and sprinkle some grated cheese on top.

This is a very hearty dish.

SUNDRIED TOMATOES WITH OLIVES OVER SPAGHETTI

You can find sundried tomatoes as well as black pitted olives in the Italian section of your local supermarket.

- 1 small jar sundried tomatoes
- 1 small jar or can black pitted olives
- ½ cup olive oil
- 1 box spaghetti
- fresh parsley, chopped
- garlic

Fry garlic in the olive oil in a pan until it becomes translucent. Add salt and pepper to taste. Drain sliced sundried tomatoes and pitted olives, then add to the garlic and oil mixture. Cook for 10 minutes.

Boil spaghetti in salted water. Strain the pasta over a small pot, reserving some pasta water to use to moisten the mixture if it becomes too dry. Mix all the ingredients together, and it's done.

This dish goes with any pasta, but I love it with spaghetti. I love making these dishes. There's nothing like the smell of fresh garlic cooking in a pan.

MY FRIEND ROXANN'S PASTA PUTTANESCA

Picture a Sophia Loren look-alike (Roxann) cooking this dish.

- ¼ cup olive oil
- 3 cloves garlic, chopped
- 1 small jar capers
- 1 jar green olives, chopped
- 1 can black olives, chopped
- 1 can plum tomatoes
- crushed red pepper to taste
- spaghetti or whole wheat pasta
- ½ teaspoon salt

In a large pan, heat the olive oil. Fry the garlic until light brown, then add all the olives and the capers. Sauté for 2 minutes. Add the can of plum tomatoes, then with a spoon, chop up the tomatoes. Add the crushed red pepper to taste. Cook for ½ hour.

In a large pot, boil water for the pasta. Add the salt to the water. When the pasta is tender, strain in a colander.

In a large bowl, mix the puttanesca sauce with the pasta. I make spaghetti with this dish or use whole wheat pasta.

This is a great Neapolitan dish that's made all the time in Roxann's house. She makes this dish great. I'll be over soon, Roxann!

NANCY'S FABULOUS CHICKEN SAUCE

- 3 28-ounce cans crushed tomatoes
- 1 medium onion
- 2 cloves garlic
- ½ cup olive oil
- 1 whole chicken, cut up (or any skinless chicken parts)
- water
- salt
- pepper

Wash the chicken in salted water until the water runs clear, then pat dry with paper towels. Season with salt and pepper to taste and place to the side.

Chop the onion and garlic very fine. Heat olive oil in a medium saucepan. Sauté onions and garlic on a medium flame. When they caramelize, add tomatoes with a little water, salt and pepper to taste. Simmer about 1 hour, then add the chicken to the sauce and cook for another hour.

This chicken sauce is great with spaghetti.

My friend Nancy is not only a good cook, she's also a good hostess and always has family and friends over to enjoy this dish. I know. I'm one of them.

CAULIFLOWER AND MACARONI

My cousin Nancy Ann (Scopi) found this handwritten recipe that her mom gave her a long time ago. She treasures it.

- 1 head cauliflower or 2 frozen bags or boxes cauliflower
- 1 medium onion, chopped
- 4 cloves garlic, chopped
- 1 small can Del Monte sauce
- salt
- pepper
- dried parsley flakes
- olive oil
- elbow macaroni or broken spaghetti
- grated cheese

If you use fresh cauliflower, break it apart and rinse well. If you use frozen cauliflower, just follow the next step. Place the cauliflower in a large pot of water and bring to a boil.

In a small pan, heat the olive oil and onions and garlic. Cook until golden brown. Pour it into the pot along with the Del Monte sauce. Season with salt and pepper to taste. Sprinkle some parsley flakes in. Cook for 1½ hours on low to medium heat. I like to cook my macaroni in the same pot, so I add either large elbow macaroni or broken spaghetti and cook till done.

Place in a large bowl and sprinkle some grated cheese on top.

When I eat this wonderful dish, I think of my aunt Winnie's cooking when we kids were all around the table ready to eat. *Buon appetito*!

MY AUNT GUSSIE'S BAKED MACARONI (PASTA AL FORNA)

When making a pot of Sunday Gravy, there's nothing like having baked macaroni for dinner. This dish can be prepared ahead of time and baked when ready to eat. Gravy (tomato sauces)

- 3 pounds ricotta
- 1 large mozzarella, sliced
- 3 eggs
- ½ cup Italian grated cheese
- 2 boxes Trio Pasta (3 different kinds of pasta in the box)

Preheat oven at 350 degrees.

In a large bowl, mix ricotta, eggs, and cheese and set aside.

Boil the pasta until al dente. Strain when done and place to the side.

In a large bowl, add gravy and the macaroni. Mix together. Make sure you add enough gravy in the bowl.

In a large baking pan, add half of the macaroni and top it with the cheese mixture and some of the mozzarella. Add more gravy on top, and repeat the layering until you are all done. Top it with some grated cheese and mozzarella. Cover with foil and bake for 30 minutes. Remove the foil the last 5 minutes.

Aunt Gussie is known in my family as Aunt Huthie. She is youngest of Grandma Jo's 18 children. She put a twist on baked ziti by add the Trio Pasta instead. Enjoy!

PASTA CARBONARA

I was introduced to this delicious dish when eating at my friends Lia and Dario's house. I loved it. I make it all the time now.

This is my version.

- ¼ pound prosciutto, sliced thick, then cut into cubes
- 1 medium onion, chopped
- 1 bag or box frozen peas
- ½ pound ricotta
- ¼ cup grated cheese
- ¼ cup olive oil
- ¼ cup water
- salt
- pepper

Heat oil in a large pan on medium heat. Add the prosciutto. Sauté on each side, then add the onions. When they become golden brown, add the peas with the water so the peas become soft. Mix together. Season with salt and pepper to taste. Cook for 15 to 20 minutes.

Boil water for the pasta. Add some salt to the water. When the pasta is done, strain in a colander with a little pot underneath it so it holds some of the pasta water.

In a large bowl, mix the pasta with the carbonara mixture. In a small bowl, mix the ricotta, cheese, salt, and pepper and slowly add a little pasta water with a tablespoon so it loosens the mixture. Add the ricotta cheese mixture to the pasta carbonara and mix well.

Serve on a platter and sprinkle cheese on top.

I love this dish with bowtie pasta or large shell pasta.

When you decide to make this dish, invite friends over. They might fall in love with this dish like I did. *Buon appetito*!

MY COUSIN CHRISSY'S MACARONI PIE

This is a fast and easy dish to make.

When making macaroni pie you can use fresh or leftover spaghetti. When you save any macaroni, always add a little olive oil and mix in a bowl so it doesn't stick. Keep it in the refrigerator no more than 2 days.

- ¼ ham
- ¼ pound salami
- 1 medium mozzarella
- 1 pound ricotta
- salt
- pepper
- dried parsley
- 1 cup grated cheese
- olive oil

Boil spaghetti al dente (not too hard or too soft; just right) in salted water. In a bowl mix the ricotta, mozzarella, grated cheese, salt, pepper, and some parsley to taste. Cut the ham and salami and mix with all the ingredients.

When your spaghetti done, strain it in a colander with a small pot underneath it so you can reserve some of the pasta water if the mixture becomes too dry. If you are using leftover macaroni you can add a little water if needed. Then mix the macaroni with all the ingredients.

In a large frying pan add a little olive oil and heat on a low to medium flame. Spread the mixture evenly in the frying pan. Cook till it is golden brown on the bottom. Place a dish as large as the frying pan on top of the pan so you can flip it over to cook on the other side. When it is done, place on a plate and cut it like a pie.

Christy's macaroni pie is just like her mom and her grandma's. She cooks old-school.

GRANDMA JENNIE'S FILETTO DI POMODORO SAUCE

- 1 medium onion, chopped
- ¼ cup olive oil
- 1 28 ounce can crushed tomatoes
- 4 leaves fresh basil
- ¼ pound prosciutto, chopped
- 1 pound pasta (rigatoni, spaghetti, or vermicelli)

In a medium-size pot, heat the olive oil and cook the onions on a low flame until they become translucent, then add the chopped prosciutto and simmer for 10 minutes. Add the tomatoes and basil, salt and pepper to taste and simmer for 1 hour.

Boil salted water for the pasta. When cooked, strain in a colander. Place in a bowl and mix the filetto di pomodoro sauce with the pasta of your choice. *Buon appetito*!

Grandma Jennie was a wonderful woman and was well loved by her family. She was also a great cook.

PASTA E PISELLI (MACARONI WITH PEAS)

- medium onions, cut up into small pieces
- ½ teaspoon garlic powder or 2 garlic cloves, cut up
- ½ cup olive oil
- 2 shakes dried oregano
- salt
- pepper
- 1 bag frozen peas or 2 large cans peas, drained
- 1 small can plain tomato sauce (optional)
- 1 can water
- pasta
- grated cheese

In a medium-size pot, heat olive oil and cook onions on a low to medium flame. When the onions turn golden in color add the garlic powder, oregano, salt, and pepper to taste. Then add tomato sauce. Add one can of water to the mixture and stir. When it starts to bubble, add the peas. I use frozen peas that are slightly defrosted. If using canned peas, drain first, then add them to the pot with 1 can of water. Cook for ½ hour on low heat and you're done.

Boil the pasta in salted water. Place a small pot underneath the strainer to reserve some of the pasta water if it's needed later.

Place in a bowl and mix all the ingredients together. If you want it soupier, add some of the pasta water to it.

Top it off with grated cheese. I love small shell macaroni with this dish; the peas slip into the shells. Or ditalini.

This is a fast and easy dish to make.

SIS'S PASTA PATATE (MACARONI WITH POTATOES)

- 5 potatoes, peeled and cut into cubes
- 1 medium onion, chopped
- ¼ cup olive oil
- 1 small can Del Monte tomato sauce
- 6 tablespoons grated cheese
- salt
- pepper
- basil
- macaroni

Peel and cut the potatoes into cubes, rinse under cold water, then pat dry.

In a large saucepan warm the oil. Sauté the onion and cook till they become golden. Then add the potatoes and tomato sauce. Fill the empty can with enough water so it covers the potatoes and cook till the potatoes are tender. Add some salt, pepper, and basil to taste, cover the pot, and continue to cook. When done, turn off the flame.

Boil water for the pasta. Cook macaroni in salted water. Strain, place in a bowl, and add the potato tomato sauce and mix together. Top it off with cheese and some more basil to taste.

I remember Sis making this dish back in the day when our kids were small. This is a hearty peasant dish.

Fritatta

FRITTATA

Barbera d'Alba
FRITTATA

MARGIE'S ZUCCHINI PIE (SQUASH)

This is a great first dish, and Margie made it the best.

- 1 cup Bisquick
- 3 cups zucchini, diced
- ½ cup vegetable oil
- 1 small onion, chopped
- ¼ cup grated cheese
- 4 eggs, beaten
- salt
- pepper
- ½ teaspoon garlic powder
- ¼ teaspoon parsley
- mozzarella, diced

Preheat oven to 325 degrees.

Combine all the ingredients in a bowl, then place in a greased 9-inch pie pan. Bake for 40-45 minutes. Eat at room temperature.

My mom and Margie were friends, her children are my friends, our children are friends, and now our grandchildren are friends—four generations. It's great, just like this hearty dish!

POTATO AND EGG FRITTATA

- 6 potatoes, peeled and diced into small pieces
- 8 eggs
- ¼ cup milk
- 1 medium onion, diced
- 3 tablespoons Italian grated cheese
- salt
- pepper
- dried parsley
- 1 cup oil

In a large frying pan, heat the oil and a little salt. Once the potatoes are cut, rinse them and then dry with paper towels. Fry the potatoes until they're golden brown on all sides. Add the onion. When golden, remove and place on a plate and drain excess oil from the pan. Return the potatoes and onions back to the frying pan.

In a large bowl, beat the eggs with milk, grated cheese, salt and pepper to taste and add to the potatoes and onions. Cook on a medium to low flame. With a spatula, check how the frittata is cooking. When ready to turn, place a plate larger than the frying pan on top. Turn it upside down, then slide it back into the pan and cook on the other side for another 5 minutes. When done, transfer it onto a plate and add the parsley on top. Cut it like a pie.

This is a no-brainer. When you feel like you have nothing in the house to make for dinner, there's always potatoes & eggs to be cooked into a great frittata.

For a little extra zing, add some roasted peppers or hot peppers to the potatoes and eggs. Oh boy, you'll love it!

A FRITTATA OF ASPARAGUS & EGGS

In any supermarket, you can find asparagus. Pick out a very thin bunch. It will work better in making a frittata.

- 1 bunch thin asparagus
- 6 eggs
- ¼ cup milk
- 3 tablespoons Italian grated cheese
- salt
- pepper
- 6 tablespoons oil

Before you separate the asparagus from the bunch, cut the ends off. Then separate and rinse under cold water. Place the asparagus in a pot and cover them with water. Cook on a medium flame till tender. Drain the asparagus and place to the side till needed.

In a large bowl, beat the eggs with milk; add the grated cheese, salt and pepper to taste. In a pan, heat the oil. Add the asparagus and cook on a medium flame till a golden color. Pour the egg mixture in the pan. When the egg becomes fluffy, it is done. Transfer it to a serving platter and enjoy.

I love making this dish. It's easy and fast. You can serve it for breakfast, brunch, or dinner.

SPINACH WITH MUSHROOM FRITTATA

- 1 bag fresh spinach or 1 box frozen spinach
- 1 small box fresh mushrooms, sliced
- 6 eggs
- ¼ cup milk
- 1 tablespoon Italian grated cheese
- ¼ cup oil
- salt
- pepper

When using fresh spinach, wash well. Place in a pot and cover the spinach with water. Cook on a medium flame till tender. If using frozen spinach, place in a pot and cook till it is all defrosted and warm.

Rinse and dry the mushrooms with a paper towel. Slice the mushrooms. Now they are ready to be cooked. In a frying pan, add the oil and fry up the mushrooms. When golden, remove from the pan, discard the oil, and put the mushrooms back in the pan.

Drain the spinach from all water and also place in the pan. Combine well. In a bowl, beat the eggs with the milk, cheese, salt and pepper to taste, then pour into the pan. When the eggs become fluffy, it's done.

This is a great frittata to make for brunch. With a crisp Italian bread, you'll be in heaven.

FRANKIE CAPPELLO'S GRANDMA JULIA'S CABBAGE FRITTATA

That's right—I said—cabbage—and it's delicious!

- 1 head cabbage
- 5 eggs
- 3 tablespoons grated parmigiano cheese
- salt
- pepper
- red hot pepper flakes
- olive oil

Take one head of cabbage, wash, and then slice it and place in a pot of water. Boil until tender, then drain the cabbage and set aside till ready to fry.

In a frying pan, add a little olive oil, just enough to coat the bottom of the pan. Heat on a low to medium flame, then add the cabbage, salt, pepper, and some shakes of hot pepper flakes to taste. Fry till golden.

In a bowl, beat the eggs with the cheese and pour the egg mixture into the pan with the cabbage. Season to taste. Increase hot pepper flakes, if desired, and then add cheese. The more you add, the richer it becomes.

Once it's nicely fried it is ready to be placed in Italian bread. Slice open the loaf of Italian bread and remove the dough inside of the bread. This will allow you more room to place the cabbage frittata inside. Slice the bread and you are ready to serve.

The Cappello family had a luncheonette on the corner of Mott and Prince Street in Little Italy for more than 30 years. When dropping off or picking up our kids from St. Patrick's School, the moms would be in the luncheonette eating their breakfast or lunch. Looking back, those were the good ole days.

Enjoy. Mangia.

Carne

ANGEL'S HEAVENLY MEATBALLS

- 2 pounds of all beef chopped meat
- 2 cloves garlic, chopped very fine
- 2½ cups Italian-style bread crumbs
- 3 large eggs
- 6 tablespoons grated cheese
- 1 handful fresh parsley, chopped fine
- salt
- pepper
- 1¼ cup olive oil

Mix all the ingredients together in a bowl. Always keep a glass of cold water on the side so when you're making meatballs, you can place a few drops of water on your hands so the meatballs won't stick when rolling. You can also add some of the water if the mixture becomes too dried. If the mixture becomes too loose, add more bread crumbs. When you finish rolling all the meatballs, you are ready to fry. Two pounds of minced meat makes 20 meatballs.

In a frying pan, add the olive oil, turn on a medium flame, heat, then add the meatballs and brown them on all sides by turning with two spoons. I place half in my Sunday Gravy and the other half in a bowl; add a spoon or two of the olive oil you just fried the meatballs with on top. Sprinkle on some parsley too.

My grandchildren love these meatballs when just fried. When I know they are coming over to eat, I don't add any meatballs to the gravy. What can I say? I'm a grandma.

MY SON GERARD'S FAVORITE DISH, STEW

Over the years, I made so many different kinds of stews—beef, veal, and pork. To be honest, Gerard never knew the difference in the meat I used. He just loves it all.

- 2 pounds beef, veal, or pork, cut into cubes
- 5 potatoes, peeled and cut into quarters
- 1 bag carrots, peeled and sliced
- 1 medium onion, chopped
- 3 celery stalks, peeled and chopped
- ½ cup olive oil
- 1 small can Del Monte tomato sauce
- 1 bag frozen peas (let the peas defrost before adding to the stew)
- 2 cans of peas, drained before adding to the Stew
- salt
- pepper
- dried parsley

Start by prepping all the vegetables and put them to the side. In a large pot, add the oil and heat on a medium to low flame. Add the meat and brown on all sides when the oil is heated. Then add the onion, celery, salt, pepper, and parsley to taste. Cook till it's translucent, then add the tomato sauce. Fill the can with water three times and stir.

Add all the vegetables and mix. Make sure you add more water to cover all the vegetables. That's what makes the sauce. Cook for 1½ hours. Place the stew in a serving bowl with crispy Italian bread on the side to dunk with. Oh boy, it's great!

To this day when I make stew and my son comes over to enjoy his favorite dish, he still doesn't know the difference in the meat. That's G.

TONY'S STEAK PIZZIOLA

Tony is a butcher and a great cook. He can slice meat as thin as paper.

- 2 cans plum tomatoes (San Marzano D.O.P. Certified)
- 3 cloves garlic, sliced thin
- 4 pieces basil, chopped
- 4-6 pieces chicken steaks (top chuck)
- ¼ cup olive oil
- salt
- pepper
- 1 pound spaghetti

In a pan, heat the olive oil on a low to medium flame. Add garlic and sauté till golden in color, then add the tomatoes. When it starts to bubble, mash the tomatoes with a fork or a potato masher so they break apart. Add salt and pepper to taste and cook for ½ hour.

Grease the bottom of another pan and brown the steaks on both sides. Add the tomatoes and cook for 1 hour till done.

Boil salted water for the spaghetti. Drain when done. Transfer to a plate, add the pizziola sauce with some basil on top. Wow!

Like my friend Tony always says, "It is what it is." Yes, it is, Tony—it's great!

COUSIN CATHY'S CHICKEN CUTLETS MARINATED IN ARTICHOKES, MUSHROOMS, AND MOZZARELLA

- 1 pound chicken cutlets
- Italian bread crumbs (I prefer homemade)
- salt
- pepper
- grated cheese
- garlic, chopped
- 1 jar marinated artichokes
- 1 jar marinated mushrooms
- large mozzarella
- 2 eggs, beaten
- olive oil

Preheat oven to 350 degrees.

Cut each chicken cutlet into three pieces, dip into the eggs, and then into the bread crumb mixture. Fry in a pan with olive oil on medium heat. Cook on both sides till golden brown. Cut up the artichokes and mushrooms and place in a bowl with the juice from the jars. Cube the mozzarella and mix with the artichokes and mushrooms.

In a pan, layer the chicken cutlets with the artichokes, mushrooms, and mozzarella mixture. Pour the rest of the juice over the chicken. Place aluminum foil over the top of the pan and bake for 25 minutes.

This dish is so delicious and smells great too. I love spending our summers together with all our family down on the Jersey shore and cooking great meals.

ROSIE'S BREADED SKINNY SAUSAGE (CHEESE AND PARSLEY)

When making this dish I think of Rose's girls, Anna, Jeanie, Connie, and Theresa.

In a pork store or your supermarket, purchase a ring of skinny sausages (cheese and parsley).

- 2 eggs, beaten
- Italian-style bread crumbs (or you can use plain and add your own seasonings)
- olive oil
- 1 ring skinny sausages

Cut the sausage into 3 pieces, dip them in the egg, then the bread crumb mixture. In a frying pan add olive oil, just enough to coat the bottom of the pan, approximately ¼ cup. Fry the sausages up. Cook till golden brown.

This dish is great with broccoli rabe on the side or pasta aglio e olio (pasta with garlic and oil).

This family goes back four generations with my family. Not many people can say that. I love them all.

COUSIN RITA'S POLLO AL FORNO (ROASTED CHICKEN)

- 2 skinless chicken breasts, cut in half
- 4 skinless chicken legs with thighs
- 1 large onion, sliced
- 2 cloves garlic, chopped
- 6 potatoes, peeled and cut into quarters
- 1 bag carrots, peeled and sliced
- 1 cup olive oil
- salt
- pepper
- oregano

Preheat the oven to 400 degrees.

Always soak the chicken in cold salted water for at least ½ hour, then pat dry. In a baking pan, add the olive oil with some salt and pepper, and then place the chicken, onions, garlic, potatoes, and carrots in the pan. Add salt, pepper, and oregano to taste. Bake in the oven for 1 hour. Transfer to a plate and serve.

Cousin Rita loves to make this dish. She said that you place it in the oven and 1 hour later it's done. How easy is that?

MY SUNDAY GRAVY

We eat early on Sunday, about 3 P.M. (continental style). It lasts all day. I love Sunday dinner with family and friends.

- 4 sweet sausages
- 4 hot sausages
- 1 pound pork
- 1 pound beef
- 1 medium onion, chopped thin
- 4 cloves garlic, chopped
- 5 28-ounce cans Tuttorosso tomatoes, crushed (or whatever tomatoes you like)
- 1 can tomato paste
- 1 cup olive oil
- salt
- pepper
- basil, fresh or dried

In a large pot, heat the olive oil. When it's warm, add your sausage, beef, and pork, searing on all sides. When everything is golden brown, add the onions and garlic. Cook till they become translucent. Add the tomato paste, then fill the tomato paste can with water and add that too. When it starts to bubble, add the canned tomatoes.

Add ⅓ of a can of water for each can of tomatoes you put in. Add a full tablespoon of salt and add pepper to taste. Chop basil, add, and stir.

Place the pot cover halfway over the pot. Cook for 2 hours on a low to medium flame and stir occasionally to make sure it doesn't burn on the bottom.

Be home on time when I put the water on for pasta. This is great with any macaroni or Di Palo's ravioli.

MEATBALL PARMIGIANO OVER RICE (RISOTTO)

When I make my Sunday Gravy with meatballs, I always make plenty so I can make this dish.

- 6-8 meatballs
- 25 ounces tomato sauce (gravy)
- 1 small mozzarella, slice thin
- ¼ cup parmigiano cheese
- parsley flakes
- salt
- pepper
- 3 Uncle Ben's boil-in-the-bag white rice or brown rice

Preheat the oven to 350 degrees.

In a pot, place the gravy and meatballs. Heat them on a medium flame till it starts to boil, then it's done. At the same time, start cooking your rice. Follow the directions on the box. When the rice is done, place it in a pan and add some gravy and mix.

Mash the meatballs with a fork and add them to the rice with the rest of the gravy. Slice the mozzarella and place on top of the mixture along with the parmigiano cheese, salt and pepper to taste, and sprinkle some parsley flakes on. Bake in the oven until the mozzarella is melted.

This dish is great during the week, especially when you have meatballs and gravy left over. In only 20 minutes you can make a great meal. *Buon appetito*!

SAUSAGE, PEPPER, AND POTATOES (FORNO) ROASTED

I love making a meal when all the ingredients are in one pan. In a pork store, butcher, or your local market you can find Italian pork or chicken sausage.

- 8-10 links sausage, separate the links
- 5 potatoes, peeled and cut into quarters
- 5 bell peppers (red, green, or both)
- 2 large onions, peeled and sliced
- 1 small can Del Monte tomato sauce
- 3 cans water
- 1 cup olive oil
- salt
- pepper
- oregano
- dried parsley flakes

Preheat oven to 350 degrees.

Wash the peppers, and then cut in half. Clean out all the seeds and slice the peppers thin. In a large pan, add the olive oil, sausage, peppers, and potatoes. Mix well. Add the tomato sauce with three cans of water and mix again. Add salt, pepper, oregano, and dried parsley to taste. Bake in the oven for 2 hours. Stir occasionally.

You'll know when it's cooked. The smell is amazing. With this dish you need crisp Italian bread. Enjoy.

COUSIN TRINA'S PORK SPARERIBS

This delicious spareribs recipe was passed down from Trina's mom, my aunt Anna. When my cousin makes this dish, she makes extra because everyone loves them!

- 18 pieces pork spareribs on the bone
- ½ bottle maple syrup
- ½ bottle soy sauce
- 10 cloves garlic, cut in half
- 2 shots scotch whiskey
- 1 large pinch black pepper

Preheat the oven to 400 degrees.

First rinse the ribs with cold water. Arrange ribs side by side in a 10 x 18 inch pan. Place the garlic between and under the ribs. Cover the ribs with cold water. Set aside.

In a bowl, mix all the other ingredients together. Add the mixture to the ribs. Marinate for 1 hour.

Bake in the oven for 2 hours, turning twice. When done, transfer to a platter and serve.

These ribs are so finger licking good you can't stop at one! *Buon appetito*!

Pesce

CALAMARI STEW

This is my sister Jojo's favorite dish. You can buy the whole calamari in your fish store and ask them to clean it and cut it for you.

- 2 pounds calamari
- 5 potatoes, cut into cubes
- 1 box frozen peas or 2 cans of peas, drained
- 1 medium onion
- 2 celery stalks, chopped
- 1 small can Del Monte tomato sauce
- salt
- pepper
- parsley flakes
- less than ¼ cup olive oil

In a large pot, add the olive oil, onions, and celery and cook till they become translucent. Then add your potatoes and tomato sauce. Cover the potatoes with water and add the peas. Cook on a low to medium flame till the potatoes are tender, then add the calamari, salt, pepper, and parsley to taste. Cook for another 15 minutes till tender. This is great with Italian bread.

My grandma Mary always made this dish. As kids, we couldn't get enough of it. My sister loves this dish. The old-timers like my grandma new how to stretch a meal.

MOM GRACE'S TRADITIONAL CHRISTMAS EVE CRAB GRAVY

- 1 dozen crabs (blue claw females)
- 4 28-ounce cans Italian plum tomatoes with basil
- ½ cup olive oil
- 4-6 garlic cloves
- salt
- pepper
- spaghetti

Clean the crabs first. To remove the back, hold the base of the crab with one hand and pull the shell away from the body with the other hand. Turn the crab over and pull on the triangular-shaped section, then lift it away. Turn the crab again and gently scrape away the gills on either side with your thumb or a spoon. Throw away the intestines, which run down the center of the back.

The "crab butter" is the yellow, mushy stuff in the cavity of the crab. Reserve it for better-tasting gravy.

Chop up the garlic into small pieces (do not crush the garlic) and place to the side. In a large pot, cover the bottom with olive oil. Sauté the chopped garlic until it's translucent, almost brown. Add your blended tomatoes and salt and pepper to taste. Allow the gravy to come to a boil, then lower the flame. Cook on a low to medium flame for at least 1 hour before adding the cleaned crabs. Cook the gravy for another hour and a half.

In a large pot, boil water for your spaghetti. Add some salt and cook the spaghetti until al dente. Place the spaghetti on a large platter and top it with the crab gravy and some crabs.

A traditional Italian Christmas Eve dinner is the Feast of the Seven Fishes. We still make this great meal every Christmas. In honor of Mom Grace my sister-in-law Ursula continues making the best Crab Gravy ever.

AUNT ANNA'S BAKED CLAMS (VONGOLE OREGANATA)

Aunt Ann makes this special dish for her family every chance she gets, and they love it. Let's start with the clams. Make sure the clams are closed when you buy them.

- 2 dozen littleneck clams
- 3 cups unseasoned bread crumbs
- 6 shakes oregano
- 3 tablespoons Italian grated cheese
- 1½ cups olive oil
- salt
- pepper

Preheat oven to 450 degrees.

Soak the clams in cold water; rinse twice. Wash the clam shells to make sure there is no sand on the shells. Place them in a pot, covering the clams with cold water, then cover the pot and steam them. When the clams open, they are ready to be removed from the pot and set aside. Reserve the water in the pot to use later.

In a bowl, add bread crumbs, cheese, oregano, salt and pepper to taste and slowly pour the olive oil into the mixture, stirring until it forms a paste.

Now the clams are ready to be stuffed. Open the shell all the way and discard the half of the shell that the clam is not in. Remove and discard the green part that's in the clams. Place the clams in a baking pan. Use a tablespoon to add the bread crumb mixture on top of the clams. When you are finished stuffing them, place a little water you reserved on top of the clams with a tablespoon for extra flavor. Bake in the oven until golden brown. Transfer to a platter and serve. Delizioso.

Dip a little Italian bread in the clam broth. It's truly unbelievable!

In a hot antipasto, you'll always find baked clams. My aunt Anna is a true Sicilian. She loves cooking fish, and baked clams are her favorite.

DEBRA'S CHRISTMAS EVE TUNA SAUCE

- 2 cans tomatoes, crushed
- 8 cloves garlic, crushed
- 4 tablespoons olive oil
- 3 cans Italian tuna fish in olive oil
- salt
- pepper
- pasta

In a large pan, sauté garlic in the olive oil. When golden brown, add tomatoes and cover the pan. Cook on a low to medium flame for 40 minutes. Lightly drain the tuna fish and add to the tomato sauce and cook for 30 minutes more, uncovered.

In a pot, boil water for your pasta so everything is ready at the same time. I serve thin spaghetti with this dish. No cheeses with fish. That's an Italian rule. Top it off with toasted bread crumbs.

In a small frying pan on a medium flame, add Italian seasoned bread crumbs and a few teaspoons of olive oil. Toast it in the frying pan till golden brown. Place the spaghetti on a platter and add the tuna sauce and mix well. Then top with the toasted bread crumbs.

This is a true Sicilian dish. It's a tradition in Debra's house on Christmas Eve.

COUSIN CHRISTINE'S BACCALÀ & RED HOT PEPPERS

This is a great Christmas Eve dish.

- 2-4 inch square pieces of baccalà
- 2 whole red hot peppers
- 2 garlic cloves, chopped
- ½ cup white wine
- olive oil

Soak the baccalà in cold water and change the water twice. Remove the baccalà, pat dry, and then flour it. Cook the baccalà in a pan that's coated with olive oil. Cook on both sides till brown. When done, remove the baccalà from the pan and place it to the side. Add the garlic, whole red hot peppers, and wine in the pan and simmer for a few minutes, then add the baccalà in the pan, cover, and simmer for a few more minutes on a low flame and you're done. This is fast and easy to make anytime.

Christine is a very good cook. She's a young mom, but can cook old-world dishes.

RED SNAPPER MARECHIARA

When buying any fish, I always ask the person behind the counter for help to clean the fish, debone it, or take the head and tail off.

- 1 good-size Red Snapper
- 1 medium jar or can black olives, pitted and drained
- 1 28-ounce can plum tomatoes
- 1 large onion, chopped
- 5 potatoes, peeled and cut in quarters
- ½ cup olive oil
- salt
- pepper
- fresh or dried basil
- oregano

Preheat oven at 350 degrees.

Before cooking the fish, give the potatoes a slight boil.

Rinse the fish with cold water before cooking. In a large baking pan, add the olive oil and place the fish on top of it. Then add onions, olives, and potatoes. Squeeze the tomatoes by hand before adding to the pan to break them up. Add a little water to the can and pour it in. Add salt, pepper, basil, and some oregano to taste. Bake for 45 minutes to an hour. You'll know when it's done. The smell is amazing.

This is a great Sicilian dish that I love making. Just dip some great Italian bread in the sauce. Oh boy, my mouth is already starting to water!

SPECIALTIA
DELLA CASA

SPECIALS

SPECIALS

PIZZA RUSTICA PIE
(SAUSAGE PIE)

This is Grandma Lina's Easter pie. This recipe was passed down to Cousin Nicholas who shared it with me.

Sausage pie:

- 5 pounds dry sausage, chopped
- 12 hard-boiled eggs, chopped
- 12 eggs, beaten
- 4 pounds grated Pecorino Romano

Dough:

- 7 eggs
- 3½ cups flour
- 1 tablespoon Crisco or butter

Preheat oven to 350 degrees.

Place sausage and hard-boiled eggs in a bowl with the cheese and mix. Beat the 12 eggs in a bowl, then pour it into the sausage mixture and mix well. Set aside till ready for use.

For the dough, place the flour on a large clean surface and make a hollow well in the center. Add the eggs in the center and mix from the outside in until it forms into dough.

Flour a rolling pin and start rolling out the dough. When dough is ready, cut into 3 pieces. You can make three pies with this recipe. Cut each piece in half.

In a greased springform pan, place the dough on the bottom and sides and fill with the sausage mixture. Place the remaining dough on top to form a lid. Poke some holes in the top with a fork to release steam.

Bake for 1 hour until golden brown.

This recipe is very dear to us, and we make it every Easter to honor Grandma Lina and Cousin Nicholas.

PAUL MESSINA'S RATATOUILLE À LA ITALIANO

- 1 medium eggplant, cubed
- 2 zucchinis, cubed
- 1 cup mushrooms, sliced
- 1 red pepper, chopped
- 1 green pepper, chopped
- 1 medium onion, diced
- 4 carrots, sliced
- ¼ cup olive oil
- 1½ cups shredded mozzarella
- 16 ounce V8 or tomato juice
- salt
- pepper
- garlic powder
- white rice

In a large skillet, heat oil. Add the peppers, onions, and carrots. Cook for 5-10 minutes. Add the eggplant, zucchini, mushrooms, and V8 or tomato juice. Season with salt, pepper, and garlic to taste.

Cover and simmer 20 minutes until vegetables are tender. Uncover until sauce thickens. Then add mozzarella until melted. Serve over white rice.

Enjoy!!!

This is a great vegetable dish. Paul's daughter Jeanine makes this dish all the time for her family.

LIZZIE'S RICE WITH EGG

This is a real old time dish that is still made in my cousin Connie house

- 1¼ cups white rice
- 6 quarts boiling water.
- 1 tablespoon package lard
- salt
- pepper
- fresh parsley
- 4 tablespoon Italian grated cheese
- 2 eggs, scrambled

Add the lard to the boiling water and let melt. Then add the rice, cheese, salt, pepper, and parsley to taste and cook on a medium flame. When the rice is soft (not mushy), turn off the flame. At this time mix in the 2 scrambled eggs. Once the eggs solidify, cover the pot and let it sit on stove for 1 hour or so. This rice dish can be made a few hours before serving.

When making these old-world recipes, you honor the past and the great moms that made them.

ROSEMARIE'S COTENNE IN GRAVY (PORK SKIN)

In a pork store or a butcher shop you'll find pork skin. Sometime it's sold in a package or ask your butcher for 4 sheets of pork skin. Rinse off all the impurities on the skin. Place in a pot and boil for 1 hour until soft. Drain the pork skin and wait till it is cool, and then slice it into pieces 2½ inches wide and 6 inches long.

- 2 tablespoons grated cheese
- salt
- pepper
- parsley, chopped or dried

Mix all the ingredients in a bowl, stuff each skin with a teaspoon of the mixture, then rool them and tie with butcher string or a toothpick. Place in a pot of your Sunday Gravy that is already cooking for about 1 hour. When you are ready to sit down to enjoy your Sunday dinner, take each one out, place them on a dish, and slice them.

Rosemarie, what a lady! When I think of her I smile. She was funny and had a great laugh. She also was a good cook. Her sons learned a lot from her and her dishes live on. This is their favorite. Cotenne in Gravy. *Buon appetito*!

ALICE'S EGGPLANT LASAGNA

Alice is my friend Lisa"s mom. She was a sweet lady and a good cook.
When making this dish you must have a pot of Sunday Gravy or marinara sauce to complete this recipe.

- 2 large eggplants
- 1 pound ricotta
- 1 cup grated cheese
- 1 cup olive oil
- salt
- pepper
- basil

Preheat the oven to 350 degrees.
Peel the eggplant and cut the ends off and discard. Slice into circles. Rinse under cold water, then pat dry. In a large frying pan, heat the oil. Add the eggplant and cook till golden on both side. When finished frying, place in a dish till needed.
In a baking pan, add some hot gravy on the bottom and place the eggplant on top, filling the whole bottom of the pan with the eggplant. Add more gravy on top. With a spoon, spread the ricotta on top along with the cheese. Repeat the layering till all the eggplant is in the pan. Top it off with gravy, cheese, salt, pepper, and basil to taste. Bake for ½ hour.
I remember when I first ate this delicious dish. It was at the Jersey shore at the Starlight Motel. We were all by the pool with the kids and Alice would be upstairs cooking her eggplant lasagna. What good times they were.

COUSIN PEGGY'S ZUCCHINI WITH MOZZARELLA

This is a great vegetable dish.

- 4 medium zucchini, cut into ¼ inch slices
- 1 medium onion, diced
- garlic clove, minced
- 1 green pepper, diced
- 14.5 ounce can tomatoes
- 2 tablespoons olive oil
- 1 medium mozzarella, coarsely shredded or 8 ounce package shredded mozzarella
- ¾ teaspoon salt
- ½ teaspoon sugar
- ½ teaspoon oregano
- ½ teaspoon basil

In a 10 inch skillet add the olive oil. Heat on a medium flame. When hot, add the onions, peppers, and garlic and cook until tender, stirring occasionally.

Add the tomatoes, zucchini, and all the seasonings. When it starts to boil lower the flame, cover, and simmer until the zucchini is tender and crisp. Cook for 15 to 20 minutes, stirring occasionally to break up the tomatoes. When the zucchini is done, sprinkle evenly with the mozzarella. Cover and simmer about 3 minutes or until the mozzarella is melted.

Cousin Peggy is known as Ms. Peg in our house. She cooks all the traditional peasant recipes that her mom, Aunt Mary, handed down to her. They are still loved to this day.

COUSIN MICHELLE'S PENNE WITH CANNELLINI BEANS & BASIL

- ¼ cup olive oil
- 2 garlic cloves, peeled and minced
- 3 cans cannellini (white beans), drained
- 2 large tomatoes, cored and cut into thin slices
- ½ cup torn fresh basil leaves or dried basil flakes
- 1 pound box penne pasta
- salt
- pepper
- ½ cup grated parmigiano cheese

Boil salted water for the pasta. In a saucepan, add the olive oil and put the heat on a low flame. Then add the garlic. When lightly golden, add the 3 cans of beans, tomatoes, basil, and salt and pepper to taste. When it starts to boil, stir and you're done.

When the water is ready for your pasta, boil it until al dente. Drain the pasta and place a small pot underneath so it can hold some of the pasta water if needed later.

In a large bowl, combine the pasta and the bean mixture and the water you reserved. Toss all ingredients together. Sprinkle with parmigiano cheese and enjoy.

Michele is Peggy's daughter. She is a young mom of three small children. Her recipe is a delicious and quick to make. It's a 30-minute meal.

CAROL'S BROCCOLI RABE

This is a dish like you never tasted before.

- 2 heads broccoli rabe
- 1 large can or box chicken stock
- 1 tablespoon butter
- 3 cloves garlic, sliced thin
- less than ¼ cup olive oil
- salt
- pepper

Wash the broccoli rabe well and cut the ends off. If the stem is thick, remove some of the leaves, not the flowers, and drain. In a medium-size pot, add the chicken broth with equal amounts of cold water. Bring to a boil, then add the broccoli robe and butter. Cook until it's tender, then remove the broccoli robe from the pot and drain in a colander.

In a frying pan, add the olive oil and garlic. When the garlic turns to a golden color, add the broccoli rabe and salt and pepper to taste. Cook for another 10 to 15 minutes until done. The smell of the broccoli rabe and garlic is amazing.

This vegetable dish is made in every Italian household. Carol loves to make broccoli rabe, and this is her favorite way of making it.

MARINARA SAUCE

This is a very simple and easy sauce to make. If you can find "Cento San Marzano peeled tomatoes D.O.P. certified," they're the best. Otherwise, any plum tomato you prefer is fine.

- medium onions, cut up
- 2 28-ounce cans plum tomatoes
- 3 cloves garlic, cut into small pieces
- olive oil
- salt
- pepper
- fresh or dried basil

In a large saucepan, add your olive oil and sauté onions and garlic on a medium flame. When they become translucent, add one can of plum tomatoes at a time. Mash the plum tomatoes with a potato masher. Mix it all together, then season with salt, pepper, and basil to taste. Cook with the cover halfway on the pan. When it starts to bubble, lower the flame and simmer for half an hour and you're done.

Marinara sauce can be use instead of meat sauce in many Italian dishes with your choice of pasta. I love it with fusilli or spaghetti.

Dolce

DULCE

GRANDMA MARY'S "LITTLE SPOON" FAVORITE DISH

This tasty dish is rice with sweet milk and chocolate (Riso-Au-Latti).

- 1 pound box Carolina rice
- 1 cup milk
- 2 or 3 teaspoons sugar
- chocolate shavings

Follow the instructions on the box of rice and decide how much you need to make. My grandma made the whole box of rice, and after cooking it, she stored it in a bowl in the refrigerator and took some out as needed.

Place some rice in a bowl. If the rice was just cooked, there is no need to heat it. If it is cold, then warm up the rice. In a small pot, heat the cup of milk on a low flame, add the sugar, and stir until it's warm. Do not boil. Pour the warm milk over the rice with some shaved chocolate and it's done.

I remember my grandma eating this for breakfast every morning. She loved it.

AUNT ROSIE'S CASSATA CAKE

- 2 packages unfilled Ladyfingers
- 3 pounds ricotta
- 1¼ cups powdered sugar
- 2 teaspoons rum extract
- 2 teaspoons vanilla extract
- ½ cup glazed candy (chocolate chips optional)
- 5 maraschino cherries
- colored sprinkles

Cake:

Line a springform pan with wax paper on the bottom and sides. Spilt open the Ladyfingers and line the pan bottom and sides over the wax paper.

Filling:

By hand or a mixer, mix ricotta and sugar lightly. Place the candy and extracts in a small dish. Mix and add to the ricotta. Blend and add the chocolate chips.

Put half in the pan. Put all but four Ladyfingers on the ricotta. Add the rest of the ricotta. Decorate the four remaining Ladyfingers in a wheel design. Put maraschino cherries in between them and dust them with colored sprinkles.

Cover with wax paper and refrigerate overnight.

Cassata is a traditional Sicilian cake. This is an old recipe my aunt Rose's mom Frances passed down to her. Every year, Aunt Rosie makes this great cake on her birthday.

COUSIN ERNIE & BETTY'S GRANDMA'S COOKIES

This is a very special cookie so keep it to yourself, if you can! This recipe for "Grandma's Cookies" is 100 years old.

- 2 sticks butter, melted
- 5 cups flour
- 1½ cups sugar
- 4 eggs
- 4 teaspoons baking powder
- 1 teaspoon vanilla extract
- 3 teaspoons brandy or vermouth
- pinch salt
- ½ cup milk
- ½ cup orange juice

Preheat oven to 350 degrees.

Cookies:

Mix flour, sugar, salt, and baking powder in a large bowl. Add eggs, vanilla, melted butter, orange juice, and brandy/vermouth in the mix.

The dough will now be sticky. Drop a teaspoon on a greased cookie sheet and bake for 15 minutes until the bottom of the cookies are light brown. Cool on a wire rack.

Icing:

- 2 cups confectionary sugar
- 1 teaspoon vanilla
- 2 tablespoons milk

Mix well and drizzle over cooled cookies. Enjoy this 100-year-old cookie recipe. Don't forget, it's our special secret!

AUNT MAGGIE'S CREAM PUFFS

Puff shells:

- 1 cup water
- 1 stick butter
- 1 cup flour
- 4 eggs

Preheat oven to 400 degrees.

Bring the water and butter to a boil over a low flame. Add flour to the mixture. Stir, then pour the mixture into a bowl. Add the 4 eggs and beat until it's smooth.

Grease a cookie sheet. Spoon the mixture onto the sheet and bake for 30 minutes. It makes about 18 cream puff shells. Cool them for 30 minutes.

Cream filling:

- 1 box instant vanilla pudding
- 1 cup milk
- 1½ cups heavy cream
- 1 teaspoon vanilla
- ¼ cup confectionary powdered sugar

Mix all of the ingredients in a bowl, then beat until smooth.

Make a slit in the puff and spoon the mixture into the shell. Sprinkle powdered sugar on top.

They're heavenly—enjoy!

URSULA'S FAMOUS STRUFFOLI

Like they say in my house, "It's Struff Time!"

- 5 pounds flour, sifted
- 18 eggs
- 3 sticks butter
- ½ teaspoon salt
- ½ teaspoon baking powder
- 9 tablespoons vanilla extract
- Approximately 1 gallon vegetable oil
- large jar honey
- candy sprinkles (nonpareils)

In a large pot, sift the flour, and then add the eggs. Make sure they're at room temperature; that's important. Melt the butter and let cool, then add to the flour and egg mixture. Add salt, baking powder, and vanilla; mix all the ingredients with your hands until it becomes dough.

Place the dough on a cutting board; keep some flour on the side in case the dough gets sticky. Take a small piece of dough and roll it as if you're making a snakelike shape. Then, with a small knife, cut the shape into quarter-inch pieces.

In a deep fryer or in a large pot, pour enough oil to fill the pan about a third of the way. When the oil is hot, fry the struffoli until golden brown.

Place in a large bowl. Heat the honey until it's warm and liquidity, then pour it over the struffoli. Coat all of it, then add the candy (nonpareils) sprinkles to the mixture. Place on a platter and serve.

This is a Christmas treat you can't stop eating.

DEBRA'S CHRISTMAS FIG COOKIES (CUCCIDATI)

These cookies are a lot of work, but delicious, which is why you only make them for the holidays.

- 3 pounds all-purpose flour
- 1 pound Crisco
- 1½ cups lukewarm water
- 2 packages dried figs (1 cup warm water and 1 cup sugar for soaking the figs). Soak overnight; drain water the next day
- 1 pound white sugar
- 1 teaspoon cinnamon
- orange rind from 1 orange
- walnuts, pecans, filberts, and almonds (all nuts in total should equal 1 cup when shelled)
- 1 container dried dates
- 1 tablespoon fresh lemon juice
- 2 cups powered sugar
- candy sprinkles

Cookie dough:

Place flour on a large board or table. Mix sugar and Crisco. Make a well in the center of the flour mixture and slowly add lukewarm water, ½ cup at a time while mixing from the outside into the well. Work the dough, folding into each side. The more you work the dough, the better the cookie. Roll and work the dough for 45 minutes.

Cookie filling:

In a food processor, blend figs, dates, nuts, cinnamon, and orange rind. It should turn into a sticky paste.

Making the cookies:

Preheat the oven at 350 degrees

Roll out the dough thin like pancakes. Place a tablespoon of filling in each one, and then roll up. The cookies can be shaped into various shapes, horns, tubes, wreaths, etc. Cut little slices into the cookies for the steam to escape.

Bake on a cookie sheet for 30 to 40 minutes until lightly browned. No need to grease the cookie sheet because Crisco is in the recipe. Let cool.

Cookie frosting:

Mix the fresh lemon juice and powdered sugar. Frost the cookie, then add the candy sprinkles.

Bake cuccidati cookies for your family at Christmas. It's worth all the effort. *Buon Natale a Tutti!*

TORTA BALLS

- 1¾ cups chopped almonds and walnuts
- 2 cups flour
- 1¼ cups sugar
- 2 eggs
- 3 teaspoons baking powder
- pinch salt
- 2 teaspoons lemon juice
- 1 teaspoon vanilla extract
- ¼ teaspoon almond extract
- 1¼ stick butter (melted)

Preheat oven at 350 degrees.

In a large bowl, mix all the dry ingredients, then add the melted butter and eggs. Mix until it forms dough. Dust a little flour in your hands so they are coated when rolling the dough into small balls, so the dough won't stick to your hands. When all is done, place the torta balls on a lightly greased pan and bake for approximately 1 hour. These torta balls are so delicious and are great for the holidays.

This is a very old recipe that was handed down to my dear friends Jane and her daughter Clarissa. Not only are the torta balls sweet, Jane and Clarissa are the sweetest people ever.

ORZATA AND LEMON ICE

- 2 tablespoons Orzata
- seltzer
- lemon ice

This is a cool summer drink for a hot summer day. Orzata is made with almond syrup. You can find it in the Italian section of your grocery store.

In a tall glass, pour Orzata. Then add some cold seltzer and stir. Top it with a spoon of lemon ice.

If you never had this drink before, let me tell you, you are missing something so refreshing. You'll love it.

ICEBOX CAKE

You can tell by the name ("icebox" cake) that this is an old recipe.

- 1 box graham crackers
- 2 boxes chocolate pudding
- 4 cups milk or low fat milk

Start by making the pudding. In a medium-size pot, heat the milk and the boxes of chocolate pudding. Stir constantly on a medium to low flame. Don't leave the pot. When it becomes thick it's done.

Open 1 pack of the graham crackers and place them on a large dish to form a square. With a large spoon, smear the pudding all over the crackers. Put more graham crackers down and repeat until there is none left. Crumble some broken graham crackers on top. Refrigerate for 2 hours.

You can also add marshmallows between the layers and on top to make s'mores. Wow!

This is my niece Stacy's favorite.